BLOOD
WORK

BLOOD
WORK

WITHDRAWN

MATTHEW SIEGEL

The University of Wisconsin Press

Publication of this volume has been made possible, in part, through support from the Brittingham Fund.

The University of Wisconsin Press
1930 Monroe Street, 3rd Floor
Madison, Wisconsin 53711-2059
uwpress.wisc.edu

Printed in the United States of America

Library of Congress Cataloging-in-Publication Data

Siegel, Matthew (Poet), author.
[Poems. Selections]
Blood work / Matthew Siegel.
    pages   cm — (The Felix Pollak prize in poetry)
ISBN 978-0-299-30404-1 (pbk. : alk. paper)
ISBN 978-0-299-30403-4 (e-book)
I. Title. II. Series: Felix Pollak prize in poetry (Series).
PS3619.I3814A6   2015
811'.6—dc23

                              2014030778

You my rich blood!

Walt Whitman
"Song of Myself"

CONTENTS

I

II

III

IV

V

I

"FOX GOES TO THE FOX HOSPITAL"

And look there he is back in the hospital
in the easy blue dressing gown, at this facility
with a delicate floral print on the walls.
He'd always had an affinity for flowers.
Healthy yet being repaired, he is back
in this gown and it is like an old costume
pulled out of a locked trunk in the attic
of bad dreams. In the gown he feels naked,
notices his softness, how his sex has never seemed

    less willing
to rise. As if there could be such a cause in this place.
He is healthy but writing a poem.
It is called "going back to the hospital" and written
in lowercase, most notably the first person "I"
which so often had stood properly capitalized
but for some reason today feels diminished.
He's writing a poem called "going back to the hospital"
but really he wishes he could draw a comic
featuring a small mammal version of himself.
His animal would be a fox, he decides, and promptly
changes the title to "fox goes to the fox hospital."

BLOOD WORK

The white sky presses a gauze pad
over my vein as the needle slips out.

The woman who draws from me smiles, always
remembers me, no matter how skinny I get.

No matter how dark the circles under my eyes,
she remembers me and how easy my veins are,

so visible, so thick, she doesn't even have to tie my arm,
but she does, and takes the smaller vein

the bigger one too easy. I don't tell her
the best to take my blood was a woman

who used to draw blood from animals,
part their fur, find their blue tap and drain.

She lets me play with my filled tubes. *Can you feel
how warm they are? That's how warm you are inside*

and I nod, think about condoms, tissues,
all the things that contain us but cannot.

AT THE COMMUNITY
ACUPUNCTURE CLINIC

the forms are long ropes for climbing
into the heaven of good health.

They are held together with a clip,
a little mouth clamped down.

There is no space to write how the cold hands
of each doctor felt against my belly.

A volunteer takes me by the wrist
to meet the acupuncturist.

She flips through my pages of blue scribbles
as I describe my complicated dream.

She wipes my forehead with an alcohol pad,
taps a needle into my third eye—

and I am almost silent now, just breathing,
as she hovers above each wrist and ankle,

a hummingbird pressing its thin beak
into flowers. My eyelids flutter each time

she taps a needle into me and when she's done,
spreads a blanket across my body.

[SOMETIMES I DON'T KNOW
IF I'M HAVING A FEELING]

Sometimes I don't know if I'm having a feeling
so I check my phone or squint at the window
with a serious look, like someone in a movie
or a mother thinking about how time passes.
Sometimes I'm not sure how to feel so I think
about a lot of things until I get an allergy attack.
I take my antihistamine with beer, thank you very much,
sleep like a cut under a band aid, wake up
on the stairs having missed the entire party.
It was a real blast, I can tell, for all the vases
are broken, the flowers twisted into crowns
for the young, drunk, and beautiful. I put one on
and salute the moon, the lone face over me
shining through the grates on the front door window.
You have seen me like this before, such a strange
version of the person you thought you knew.
Guess what, I'm a stranger to us both. It's like
I'm not even me sometimes. Who am I? A question
for the Lord only to decide as She looks over
my résumé. Everything is different sometimes.
Sometimes there is no hand on my shoulder—
but my room, my apartment, my body are containers
and I am thusly contained. How easy to forget
the obvious. The walls, blankets, sunlight, your love.

[AND SOMETIMES I KNOW
I'M HAVING A FEELING]

And sometimes I know I'm having a feeling
but I don't want to have a feeling so I close up
like a book or a jacket or a sack that holds
a body. Don't mind me, I'll just be dead in here,
you can drag me wherever you want, the body
seems to say. You laugh like a little silver moon.
You laugh like the moon on water ignored
by necking lovers. You say you don't like that word
because something so sweet should not call to mind
giraffes, but I love the word "necking," the way it twists
in on itself, like what I do to you when I want
to disappear in you, leave the sack of my body
strewn on the shore of you. Sometimes I'm inside
the sack and then sometimes I am nothing more
than the stitching that keeps it from bursting.
Sometimes I carry the sack and sometimes the sack
carries me. I only know the difference sometimes.
Do you ever feel like it's difficult to figure out
what you're feeling? I have that all the time, especially
when I look out a window or at your open face
across from me in bed, or your closed face
when I see the quiet pain you contain, or which
contains you. I know you're more than that
frown that makes your face resemble a fist
with gorgeous black hair. I know you contain more

than the reaction to my words or my body.
Some of us have to learn to love with hands
interlocked, but each with our own hand.

[THE BOY WITH THE BLACKBIRD STITCHED OVER HIS HEART IS SAD]

The boy with the blackbird stitched over his heart is sad
he stands even though there is a bench behind him he stands
and looks at the floor, at Mother's ankles, away from the cut-
open sun that shimmers his hair. The bird stitched to his shirt
is not quite over his heart, but close enough, for sure over
his esophagus. The bird does not chirp, it perches on a button
it hums and nudges the boy's chin, his lips.
The boy stands not paying attention to his brother barely
inside the frame, his brother who sits with an arm around
a cat, his fingers stroking its kitten. The boy does not
pay attention to the window behind him which frames
a tissue standing straight up from its box, a few flowers
tucked into a small vase. The boy does not pay attention
because he has a bird on his chest that whispers to him
in the night, it flies around the room and comes back,
flies around his heart and settles right there on his shirt.
The boy with the bird on his chest curls his fingers, cannot
look into the camera lens. The boy stands there at attention
as the world has instructed him previously and will continue.

after a photograph by Larry Towell

THE ELECTRIC BODY

changes like a sky bleeding peach,
gray feathers and smoke—

        a body circular as the earth,

water and air,
rivers surging through.

*

Eight quarts
of blood

run laps inside
my body

arrive, leave
like a Psalm

the chorus
to an electric body–

song.

*

At sixteen something broke inside me
in the gym locker room. I'd never wear

those shorts again. Breath swept
from me

mist pulled
from boiling water.

*

My body is a series of bodies:
now & before

I realize how much blood
moves within me.

I wear this living skin—
wear it in the sunlight,

in the forest, in the city—
wear it like a suit

of metal, a suit of gauze—
my face of abalone, of straw

assembling, trembling
apart in the water.

*

Dr. Green wore black vests,
had no skull. I could see the folds of his brain.

My mother told me how he kissed with his mouth
open. Waiting in my underpants

in his office I stole gauze pads, tape,
a plastic model of an inflamed colon

to show my mother how I felt inside.
It was hard to make her laugh back then.

His eyes, I really remember, sad like a horse's eyes,
ringed with dark just the same.

*

Then came Dr. Chen who quietly examined the surface
of my tongue that day in his California office.

He laid me out on a table, touched my ankles,
wrists, neck with his starfish-hands.

At the bottom of his clear mug,
a bag of green tea bled into hot water.

He marked Chinese characters on a chart.
He told me even in English, I wouldn't understand.

*

The first time I take the shot, I jab myself
in the side of the stomach, over an old wound

invisible to me. I shake a little as I pinch the skin
and wait for my body to finish sipping

from the thin needle. The doors to my body swing
open. Air rushes through the hallways

all the lights flickering on.

*

I want to make music
from what isn't broken,

make memory disappear
like medicine absorbed

in the blood. I want to whittle a whistle
from my bones. Tenderize the sky.

Smear with my thumb
God's purple night makeup.

Hello, old pain. So strange
how you resemble my old face.

Won't you come inside?

II

AT THE EDGE OF THE FIELD

I part the petals of a flower,
run my finger along its stamen.

I push the clouds
back up into the sky.

At the edge of not speaking, the edge of Let's
keep going let's do it This way.

The edge of Yes.
The edge of a flame's heat that encircles its burning.

At the edge of my bathtub
reintroducing your name to my mouth.

My living warmth at the edge of a field
that represents you, a field under stars.

A field, all yellow flowers glowing.
So much buried beneath, roots and minerals

hard, cold things. No matter.
I enter the field. The field contains me.

[THE HEART IS A DUMBWAITER]

The heart is a dumbwaiter
rising to the kitchen.

Or maybe it is a coffee can,
a hole punched through with a nail

and a word is simply a long string
you pull through and knot.

It is a penny tossed into the electric fountain
of the mall food court. How glamorous

all this appears from the outside.
Copper wire in the walls

of the gutted house. The body's rich
secret, the body's dirty truth.

A stairwell to the roof, a stairwell
to the dark basement.

It descends like a bag of grapes dropped
from a high window into waiting hands.

[MY PILLS DOZE UNTIL
I WAKE THEM]

My pills doze until I wake them
on the shelf

behind the bathroom mirror,
the one I see myself in

curled over, whimpering,
eyes dark and heavy

like lakes at night.
My pills doze until I shake them

and they dissolve inside me,
make complicated arrangements

with my biology.
They sleep and I take them,

gathered in the cup of my hand.
They tick against my teeth

and I hold my hand over my mouth
as if to shut them up.

THE HEATER REPAIR-WOMAN

The heater repair-woman takes the stairs
two at a time as she enters my apartment,
her belt heavy with surprises.

She drops to her knees, pulls the wall unit apart,
and with a tube in her mouth
blows into the cavity.

She taps the small pipes with a wrench,
wakes up the entire neighborhood.
She does not have the tools she needs

to look inside and I think of the mysteries
of my own body. I lie back in bed and she shouts
to me from the hallway

that she's seen heaters in worse shape,
but these chambers are choked
with white ash. I drowse

and her voice holds me
between sleep and wakefulness.
It is the wakefulness I love.

SUCH IS THE SICKNESS

I read her a poem by Robert Duncan. We're stoned and she's
      eating pizza.
I'm in something that resembles love and she doesn't want
      to be dating anyone right now.

All the flame in me stopt / against my tongue

I read that line three times aloud and she nods at me.
I look up at the corner of the room, down at my water glass
      beading
on the counter next to the oregano.

               She is not going to love me, not even after
we stood at the bluff
at the edge of the continent on a foggy day overwhelmed
      with the enormity
of the ocean rocks and the sound they made when the
      muscular waves
pulled them in, clacking into one another underwater.

Her face was an open window and my face was an open
      window
and we were the same house and for a moment the sun
      seemed to shine through us.

My heart was a stone, a dumb
unmanageable thing in me, I read

and she shakes and shakes the oregano onto her pizza,
asks me what I am thinking about. *Such is the sickness
of many a good thing.*

I am thinking about walking out of here

leaving her with a greased paper plate but I don't say that.

WHAT I FAIL TO MENTION

You press a scar on my back
with your finger

releasing memory into my body
like blood in water,

curled tea in hot water
uncurling. You ask about the small circles.

I tell you the sky broke
and some pieces fell on me

as I slept shirtless in the sun,
my belly against the grass.

Each opens a small door in my body
if you touch with your tongue.

I don't say any of this. I kiss your neck,
you turn away, hand me my shirt.

From your stoop I watch the sun
seep into the sky, a spill

that can never be cleaned.
My mouth opens and closes in the cold.

AT THE VIETNAMESE
MASSAGE PARLOR

You say nothing when I walk in
but *take off clothes, keep underwear.*
Keep underwear, you say twice more
with your back turned to me soaking
and wringing a towel in hot water,
steam rising up around your head.
The water from the towel drips
into a large bowl. My belt buckle clinks
against the tile, the table creaks
as I lie down in my underwear.
The light clicks off and you approach me.
Your hands worker's hands. The lumps
in my back stones you lift from dirt,
bows you loosen using all your fingers.
You are a drawer removed from its dresser
like me—partially filled, partially empty.
I want to hold your emptiness
but I did not pay to touch; I paid
to have you press the breath from me.
I sing to you but you do not understand.
I tremble in this room, warm enough.
You whisper *excuse me* when it is time
to turn over, but I hear *kiss me*
and lie there not breathing at all.

[MOTHER PUTS ON
MY LIPSTICK]

Mother puts on my lipstick
standing behind me, dragging the lipstick
across my lips as if they were her own.
Her free hand steadies my face. It's the red
of her nails I want on my mouth,
the nails so lacquered they catch the flash
of my camera and hold it steady.
Mother puts on my lipstick and I stare
into the mirror, my lower lip glowing
beneath her hands. Her hands that are all of her
and that hold me this way, like she wants me.

after a self-portrait photograph by Elinor Carucci

ON THE WAY TO THE AIRPORT I FAIL TO TELL MY FATHER I LEFT SOME MEAT IN THE REFRIGERATOR.

Sirloin my mother cooked hastily for me
as I was packing up my things once again.
It dripped red as she pressed it to my lips
when I leaned down to kiss her goodbye.

I never knew watching someone eat
could be a kind of prayer, but she was praying
as I chewed whatever meat she gave me;
meat cooked while leaning on crutches,

still too much weight on her busted foot.
Kissing me goodbye she tried to stand
but wavered like a house being punished by wind,
a house stripped of shingles.

And my father pulls off into the gas station
to fill his empty tank. The flow of gas sounds
like the flow of blood. The same pressure.
The same insistence. The same rush and fill.

III

[WHAT WORLD ARE YOU IN, MOTHER, WHEN YOU SLEEP]

What world are you in, Mother, when you sleep
and when you are falling asleep? What world
contains you as you toast an English muffin,
call it both breakfast and lunch? What world
as you look out the window and notice it's raining?
You brush your teeth and look in the mirror
of the medicine cabinet but let's not talk about that here,
for the sake of love, Mother, I will only consider your face,
your sleeping face lit by the television at night.
Alone like so many mothers, I'm sure, but I cannot see
anyone else with such clarity as on this night
when I visit you. You are sleeping and your lips
part a little as you exhale in little puffs,
your body's engine running like an American car.
I am only your son, I can only watch for so long
until I have to lie down on the couch
you set up for me with blankets
and pillows stripped from your own bed.

WEATHER OF THE BODY

I was getting stoned in the kitchen with my mother
when my sister, wrapped in clouds, filled the room
with lightning.

Her words moved through my stoned mother
like a wire pulled through a lump of clay,
her body held together

by the terrycloth belt of her bathrobe.
Each vertebrae in my spine tingled like radio static.
I closed my eyes, my teeth fell out.

I ran outside to my car, startled a bird
sleeping beneath the undercarriage.
It fluttered up and out as if from within me—

its wings, so frenzied with movement,
broke apart right then and there:
my mother grieving her failed marriage,

hail cascading down her face, my sister,
her mouth wide open and electric shouting at me—
you don't live here anymore, Matthew, you don't understand.

LIFE GUARDING

My sister tells me to turn up whatever it is I'm listening to
because Mom is sobbing in her bedroom with the door half
    open
and we're in the kitchen trying to fix our dinners. I fight
with my father the next morning about it. He comes down
from his home office, silently slices me cantaloupe. At
    the pool
I open one umbrella, fumble with locks. I don't water
    the plants
because it rained. I drop little white pills into test tubes,
    crouch
and wonder if I could reassemble my mother, if the day
    could loosen
its grip. I sift a dead bird out of the bright water with a net.
I chase the opened umbrella as it lifts, tumbles through the air.

FASTER

My mother is sobbing again
behind her bedroom door,
the phone's hot battery

against her cheek. Her ex-fiancé
is dying; she still phones him.
She tells me he spends his day dragging

an oxygen tank across the floor.
She sniffles, begins
to blow-dry her hair. Or maybe

it's my sister, who just switched
on the radio—rock music,
but soft. I would shout

if I thought it might help.
I would submerge the phone in water
if I thought it might take him from her faster.

IN THE DENTIST'S CHAIR

Nancy asks me if I've been stressed as she digs a hook
    between my teeth.
With her hands in my mouth I gurgle and grunt as she says
You've been grinding. She scrapes a tooth and my eyes liquefy.

She asks if I've been flossing in that way that lets me know
she knows I haven't. The blood I spit into the little plastic
    sink
proves it. I tell her I flossed before I came, she replies
    Not good enough

and slaps a lead vest over my genitals. *Bite down. Turn your
    head*. She
positions a machine next to my face, turns the light off and
    leaves. It beeps
and clicks and she flips the light back on, yanks the film from
    my mouth,

holds the tiny X-ray to the light. She grips my jaw and looks
in the cave of my mouth as if she's about to crawl inside.
    Humming,
she shoots a needle full of novocaine into the softest part
    of me.

I breathe loudly as she hushes me with an unexpected
    tenderness
that reminds me there is nothing cruel or unusual about this.

SOAP

Tiny black bits float in the water pitcher
and I think *How does she live this way?*

I drink a whole glass down, the water
cold against my teeth, all the fillings cooling

in their drilled homes. From my sister's bedroom
she sighs every time she leans to fix the sheets.

She drags the space heater in by its cord,
it rolls over the dog's paw, he yelps,

she yelps. I want to make her better
but it's not my job.

I need, at least, to make her smile,
so I order her a bar of soap from the Internet

with her favorite political commentator's face
printed on it. Every night she watches him

from beneath her electric blanket,
admires his square jaw, square shoulders,

perfect pepper-salt hair. He leans toward her
almost falling out of the television.

MOTHER WASHES ME
IN THE TUB

A forearm laid across my chest and throat,
I'm pinned against her body in the clear hot water,

every inch of its surface moving.
She holds me as she holds herself,

holds nothing, my body, straining to twist
from her grip, almost unrecognizable.

She washes me in the tub and my fingers reach out
toward her camera that clicks on its tripod

like a blackbird. My fingers reach outside her reach.
Mother-bird, head bowed above me,

your wings pin me down, and I make such a racket
I almost cannot hear you sing.

after a self-portrait photograph by Elinor Carucci

MATTHEW YOU'RE LEAVING
AGAIN SO SOON

please take these pens I have all these pens
for you all with caps on them and pen holders
I have all these pen holders large and plastic

I know they won't fit in your bag I'll mail them
take this umbrella this sweater these socks
they're ankle length like you like them

and soup take this soup I froze four batches
in Tupperware four batches of broth and chicken
and carrots and celery frozen in the freezer

they will keep you healthy my son
my liver take my liver to help clean your blood
I'll fly to you I'll come to you tomorrow

you used to cling to my ankle and I would
drag you across the floor please
pack me in your suitcase take me with you

IV

WATCHING CHRISTMAS TREES BURN, OCEAN BEACH

I am thinking of my childhood on fire.
No, I am wondering how a child could forgive
a parent as black smoke bends
toward the parking lot. It turns
the whole dim sky orange, erases the stars.
But stars are behind smoke
like the image of my father in my face.
I need him to step out but he will not,
I need him to get off the couch
but the memory is obstinate. I want to burn
the couch instead of these piles of pine,
burn the television, burn the memory
of a father who threw baseballs into the clouds
until the clouds were heavy.
Who made a fortress for himself
on the couch or deep inside a telephone
while Mother bolted every lock
inside herself and slept. Tree after tree dragged
through the sand and thrown onto the fire
makes an ordinary sky seem beautiful enough,
until the police, who do not even get out
of their cars, shine their bright beams, which say
it's ten o'clock, time to return home.

FOR BRYAN, 13, WHO SLEEPS THROUGH LI-YOUNG LEE

Normally I would snap my fingers
behind your ear but it's summer
and I understand why you are sick
of poems. Normally, I would wake you
with my teacher voice and ask
Is there a problem, Bryan?
But instead I watch you, head down
on the cool desk, your back rising,
falling with each breath, as if
you were my son on vacation,
tired of temples. The classroom is dark
and warm like the inside of a flower.
The projector hums like your mother.
Love the questions themselves, I said
to you earlier, and you looked up at me
in that way children look up at adults.
I want to tell you I too know
what it means to eat lunch alone
at a big table watching girls laugh,
sip cold blue slush through thick straws,
what it means to watch soup steam rise,
to breathe it in, look for figures
in the noodles, how it feels to force-feed
the last few golden mango chunks at dessert.
Bryan, I am not going to tell you
how lovely you are asleep on your desk,

how one day, maybe you might turn into a man
who looks at a boy sleeping in his classroom
and instead of chastising him
wants to touch his hair.

THE GIRL DOWNSTAIRS IS CRYING

The girl downstairs is crying and no
this is not about my mother, not at all,
as the sobs rise through the floor like
nothing else. The girl downstairs is crying
and I hear the echo of my mother's small room
miles away in New York, remember
how I heard her through my thickest sheets,
through the fingers blocking my ears,
heard her rise, the tender nob of her body
turning and turning without opening any doors
to any place. Tonight I listen from my bed,
as if the girl's cries are a radio show in a language
I understand but cannot speak. Though
I fall asleep to the sound of a stranger's sobbing
I'm home.

AT THE FARMERS' MARKET

Sunburnt shoulder blades!
Knives big as my face!
Zongo juice, a man tells me, will cure your everything!
He tells me of a man with Crohn's Disease
on the toilet & the verge of suicide, saved!
I buy a bottle, rub it all over my body!
I'm cured of everything: sadness, rickets,
& happiness too! Gee whiz/willickers!
Raw red meat bleeding on brown wax paper!
Fish that smells like fish!
A skinny boy with thick glasses, freckles, and a faded blue tee
tells me to try a strawberry!
Says the little ones are the most sweet!
I bought some and now the little ones taste like tart-bombs!
My mouth has been bombed with tart-berries!
I lift my tongue and discover where spit comes from!
I ate a million berries until I pooped!
& pooped until I couldn't!
I've never been so afraid in my life!
Berries so many berries!

LOVE PARADE

Down Market Street today there is a love parade
and I fear my body incapable of loving.

The girls dance in the streets
with bangles and sunglasses and suns

painted on their stomachs. It is unbearable.
The bank teller hands me my money, winks

thinking perhaps I too will go to the parade,
find someone to wrap my love around

like clean paper. Outside, the sunlight feels good
on my skin but I walk back into the house.

The sunlight feels good but I sit in my room
with the blinds drawn searching the computer

for my friends who will make me feel better
about this world that I must be grateful for.

BY THE FLOWERS AT
THE SUPERMARKET

At the supermarket the floral woman asks me
if I need any help. *Complicated question*, I reply

and spend a few minutes dipping my face
into the rising breath of the flowers.

I'm ready to be helped now, I tell her
and she asks what my intentions are.

I'd like the girl to see that I can have flowers
inside a big glass jar on my coffee table just to look at

and I don't need them to be beautiful,
just a little scent in case she does not return.

Of course she knows which ones, her picks
so quiet, subtle, barely looking like flowers,

and the magenta glows among the shades
of green and feathery gray. She lays the bunch

on tissue, ties them together. The serrated knife
whets its metal teeth on the lengths of stems

leaving the ends angled, open-mouthed.

WITH MY FACE BURIED IN SUPERMARKET FLOWERS I SPENT THE ENTIRE EVENING.

My telephone failed to reach you so I left
the flowers in my car under the streetlight.
They glowed there like something sealed up inside me.

I brought them into the house where I untied the ribbon
that held them together, put them into the freezer.
Hours later I wanted them for me, but by then

the petals were weak, translucent in kitchen light.
So I walked them out the back door,
threw them under the house. The next day they were

mostly rotted in mid-bloom. I split the stem of one,
ran my thumb along the wet insides. They were alive,
the irises, somehow still blue as veins.

[IT'S TRUE WHAT YOU'VE HEARD ABOUT MY MOUTH.]

It's true what you've heard about my mouth.
Radio signals in the fillings, sparks in the snap
of mints in the dark. I am silent and afraid
and find comfort in world news watching
everything blow up except my apartment.
I'm aware this is very American of me.
This is all too much for me to understand.
When there is silence with my friends I say stupid shit,
I can't help it. I look at people a second too long
and we both get uneasy. I move vegetables
around the surface of a hot grill with my hands
and never learn any lessons. Of course not.
Of course the alligator in the pond is going to snap
when I toss a twig into the water. I have always been
that person. Self-consciousness presses its moist palm
against my neck. I smoke on my stoop to lift myself up
like the smoke. I didn't eat one apple this weekend
and yes, I did feel like something was missing.
My friends were here instead on my inflatable mattress
and now they are gone and something else is missing.
Who needs to see this apartment anyway with the purple walls
and orange door? Lazy ceiling fan and quiet stoop,
palm trees that look alien to me still, as a heavy breeze
shakes rain from their fronds. But what about continuity?
I'm always forth and back. Always counting
on my fingers. Avoiding complicated math or science.

47

The late-night TV ads are for the sick, weak-willed,
and dying to chat for a low fee. I'm dying to chat
for a low fee as I eat my late-night snack of chips,
golden raisins, snap peas. I'm the one
with a phone in my hand paying to tell you this.

OVERLOOKING THE CITY

The city lights up one kitchen at a time.
A woman sits by me,

I can smell the mint on her breath, it mingles
with the colors bleeding into, out of the sky.

I'm not sick, sitting here in the twisted tower
of the de Young Museum.

Praise God for beauty without barbed hooks,
without needing a woman's hands.

No, I am not hurting in this moment.
I am memory's lips sewn shut.

The sky is pink now, red in some places
and the red does not remind me of blood.

I do not see it on the cars, the woman's lips.
It does not hurt, finally, the sun's rays

reaching out all around, almost reaching
even me, surrounded here and alone

in this tower overlooking the city
in which I am trying to live.

V

[AND BECAUSE THE WANT IS
THE SIZE OF A BUILDING]

And because the want is the size of a building
you decide you're going to build a city within
yourself, a city that is all sunsets reflected off windows
of the buildings where the people work. The buildings
where the people work and pretend they are in the sky
or closer to some idea of heaven. She is your idea
of heaven. She is your idea and so she is the mortar,
the bricks, the girders, the cement, the wires
running up and down like electric veins and this hum
is her song. You've been hearing it all along
especially when it rains and the cars drive and the people
walk the streets and it is like her breathing, her heavy
breathing when she turns over in bed. It is the rain
and it is when she sleeps and when she cannot sleep.
This is your city, it is the city of her body beneath
her many and varied sheets, which still bear traces
of your loving. And so the city. And so the buildings.
The eternal hum and rise. The comb you honey yourself
into. And because the want is the size of a building
you make many more buildings, taller buildings
on top of which you can see the curvature of the earth,
far more slight than that of her body and look there,
something that is not her. It is your city, you're making it,
you're even opening up a small cupcake shop, you stir
eggs into flour all day, wear an apron, say *Hey there,
cupcake* to every new customer. Look how much

you're enjoying life in this city of your making
where suddenly your want is just another building.
Where your love glistens like all the others
and you almost forget whose body it is all made of.

LIVING WITH YOU

I am maddened by the crashing of dishes in my sink
as I pull out the biggest pot looking for the strainer.
I've got too many needs for a month like November.

I want to pen a sign onto my chest
Help me, I cannot sleep or stand up, would you
touch a stranger's face?

My body is a tunnel filled with smog,
but I keep the windows open anyhow.
I keep the windows open anyhow and inhale

the smell of wet leaves as they circle
after a knock to the head.
My brain is a couch on the sidewalk, springs

splitting through, not worth the repairs. Low music
comforts me, Bob Dylan with a pillow
over his face. His harmonica: the reeds,

the hum of solitary breath.

IN THE BATHROOM

I hold small echoes
in my hands. Each breath

a storm cloud. It is morning,
I dream no longer.

It is morning, an alarm
chips away at me.

My hands grip my knees.
I'll wash them and wash them.

I lean into my body like a needle,
like a losing argument.

I cannot look at my living blood
in this tiny world where I am

more alone than being born,
more alone than dying.

[HE'S LOOKING FOR ANSWERS HE'S LOOKING FOR THE ROUGH DARK]

He's looking for answers he's looking for the rough dark
that can only be found in music when the sky is so bright
outside insisting its way in through the round windows
through the crack between the swinging bar doors and
    the floor
light persisting like a hangover no number of beers can kick
tiles torn up around the jukebox which hums like an animal
he's looking for solace and lifts one hand to place against
the smudged glass as he decides which backlit button
his finger will press his hair shines but it is black it shines
but only a little his shirt is meant for nighttime it blurs
even though he's still it blurs because his head is down
and he is only looking at the jukebox but he is the saddest
person in the world who can still bear music who can still
fill the silences in his life with dancing even though
the dance floor is empty scuffed filled with difficult light

after a photograph by Robert Frank

[IN THE KITCHEN MOM STANDS
WITH HER BACK TO ME]

In the kitchen Mom stands with her back to me
facing the window, a joint between her fingers
entranced by Enya. I ask her why she's crying
when I see a single wet trail on her cheek.

She says it is not a tear but I touch it with my finger
and taste it. *It tastes like a tear*, I say, but she smiles
and passes me the joint. *Isn't it beautiful*, she says,
it's in Gaelic, her smile as real as her pain.

Her pain that touches my chest with its fingers.
I almost want to hold the fingers but I don't, instead
I puff the joint, look out the window beside her. Rain
all day until now, the sky a dark cream color

almost backlit with orange—mist tumbles
over wet black pavement. Her eyes, switched-off
depositories for this light, tell a story I cannot bear.
The memory of him rises with this music
and she smiles as if the hurt is the balm.

[HE'S BECOME TOO LARGE FOR HIS CHILDHOOD BED]

He's become too large for his childhood bed
and yet he's drawn here in his dreams
with a charcoal pencil on a sheet of butcher paper.
He is sketched in, gently at first, that little cross
that will be his face, then the swipe that will be
his shoulders. The drawing is from the point of view
of the ceiling. As if a ceiling could look down like God
who never looks down. He's praying and in the prayer
he asks to mean the prayers he's praying,
to mean his prayers more than when he's drunk
and vomiting and that's all there is to do except expel.
He wants to expel here in this drawn bed,
he wants the acupressurist to rub that point
in his wrist that releases all the repressed feelings,
because he feels pressed against the bed
with the giant hand of the ceiling, pressing
his entire body like a tea bag in hot water.

MOTHER DRIVES ME IN THE RAIN

She's going fifty and you can see
the taut tendons in her wrists,
her wrists emerged from her black fur coat
to suck up all the light in the world.
Her fingernails are dark red
like the switched-off hazard lights.
It is past noon, the sky so gray,
just a bit of blue mixed in, so thin,
so cold. Mother drives me in the rain
and we must be going to the airport
of dreams, it doesn't matter what station
the clock radio is tuned to. It doesn't matter
what things we have lost. There is a green sign
in the distance, it tells us where we are going
and how many miles till we get there.

after a photograph by Elinor Carucci

RAIN

I thought I knew desperation until I found myself
tightening my asshole like a bolt,

gripping the banister and crossing both legs,
knees shaking.

I tried to read a poem on the toilet,
tried not to think about how many quarts

of blood surge through the body, how many gallons
of water it takes to dilute them. I sat, forearms across belly,

allowed the bright red life to leave me.
This isn't the first I've spoken of this

but I can't stop thinking about all the mouths
that keep so tight the lips throb,

hands that ball into tight forever-fists.
I am always halfway

to becoming ok with this.
But I can eat sweet dates,

steer a car with one knee.
I can look out my window and see grass

glowing green in rain and streetlight—
so many bright beads of water.

ACKNOWLEDGMENTS

Thank you to the editors of the following journals in which some of these poems first appeared, sometimes in slightly different forms: *Cimarron Review*, *Connotation Press*, *DIAGRAM*, *Gigantic Sequins*, *Forklift Ohio*, *Indiana Review*, *The Journal*, *Lo-Ball*, *The Lumberyard*, *Mid-American Review*, *Ninth Letter*, *Paterson Literary Review*, *Pebble Lake Review*, *RedWheelbarrow*, *The Rumpus*, *Salt Hill*, *Saw Mill Online*, *Southern Humanities Review*, *Southern Indiana Review*, *Spinning Jenny*, *Toad*, *TheThe Poetry Blog*, and *Tusculum Review*.

"Matthew you're leaving again so soon" was a special mention for the Pushcart Prize.

I am eternally grateful to my family for unceasing love and encouragement.

Thank you to my teachers and friends, whose guidance and support helped carry me through the years of writing these poems: Kim Addonizio, Amanda Auchter, Eavan Boland, Devon Branca, Abby Caplin, Mark Doty, Ken Fields, Maria Mazziotti Gillan, Eddie Gonzalez, Bob Hicok, Tony Hoagland, Natalie Jabbar, J. Kastely, Sophie Klahr, Peter Kline, Eric Kocher, Keetje Kuipers, Dorianne Laux, Brittany Perham, Leigh Phillips, Christine Potter, D. A. Powell, Martha Serpas, Cody Todd, Brian Trimboli, and Betsy Wheeler.

The writing of this book was made possible with gifts of time, instruction, and generous financial support from the Wallace Stegner Fellowship at Stanford University, the Graduate Program in Creative Writing at the University of Houston, the Inprint Foundation, the Center for Writers

---

63

at Binghamton University, and the Stadler Center for Poetry at Bucknell University.

Thank you, Lucia Perillo, for believing in this book.

Thank you, Ronald Wallace and the University of Wisconsin Press.

THE FELIX POLLAK PRIZE IN POETRY

Now We're Getting Somewhere • David Clewell
Henry Taylor, Judge, 1994

The Legend of Light • Bob Hicok
Carolyn Kizer, Judge, 1995

Fragments in Us: Recent and Earlier Poems • Dennis Trudell
Philip Levine, Judge, 1996

Don't Explain • Betsy Sholl
Rita Dove, Judge, 1997

Mrs. Dumpty • Chana Bloch
Donald Hall, Judge, 1998

Liver • Charles Harper Webb
Robert Bly, Judge, 1999

Ejo: Poems, Rwanda, 1991–1994 • Derick Burleson
Alicia Ostriker, Judge, 2000

Borrowed Dress • Cathy Colman
Mark Doty, Judge, 2001

Ripe • Roy Jacobstein
Edward Hirsch, Judge, 2002

The Year We Studied Women • Bruce Snider
Kelly Cherry, Judge, 2003

A Sail to Great Island • Alan Feldman
Carl Dennis, Judge, 2004